Rats

By Avery Blalock

Library For All Ltd.

Library For All is an Australian not for profit organisation with a mission to make knowledge accessible to all via an innovative digital library solution. Visit us at www.libraryforall.org.au

Rats

First published 2019

Published by Library For All Ltd
Email: info@libraryforall.org.au
URL: http://www.libraryforall.org.au

PNGAus Partnership

This book was produced by the Together For Education Partnership supported by the Australian Government through the Papua New Guinea-Australia Partnership.

Rats
Blalock, Avery
ISBN: 978-1-925932-51-5

Images sourced from Pixabay.com, Pexels.com, Maxpixel.net, Flickr.com, Wikipedia.com, Goodfreephotos.com, Freepik.com under a CCO license.

A rat is a type of rodent. Rats are found all over the world.

Rats can live anywhere that humans can live. They are found in houses, shops and offices. They also live in tropical rainforests, deserts and grasslands.

There many different types of rats. They can be large or small and can be many different colours.

The largest rats are Gambian
pouched rats.

Osgood's Vietnamese rat is one of the smallest rats.

Rats have furry bodies, large ears and long tails.

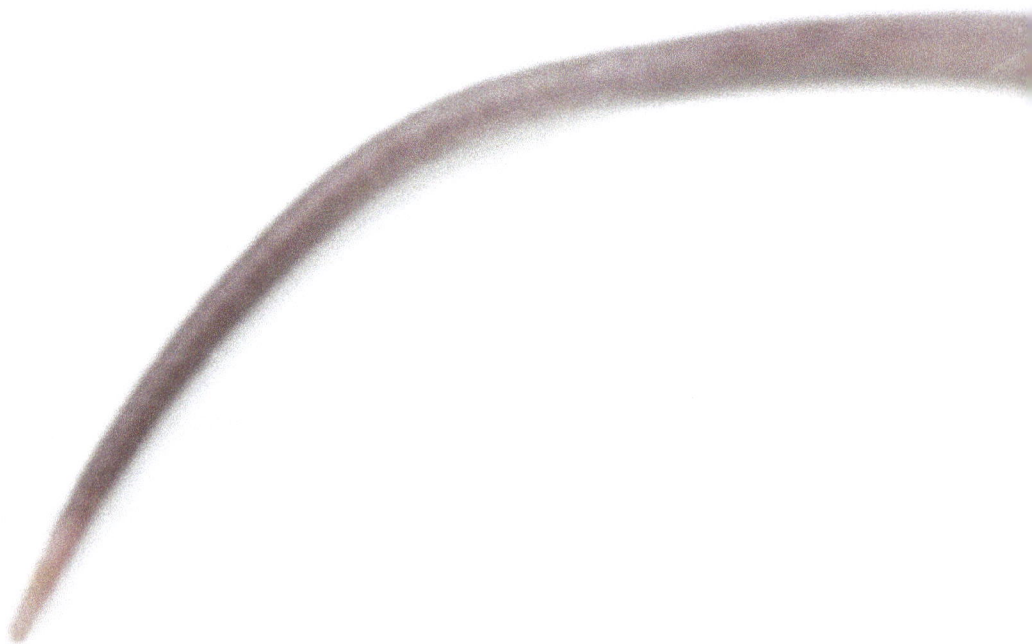

Rats have many predators,
including cats, dogs, foxes, snakes
and owls.

Rats live in colonies and have many babies. One rat can have over 100 babies in a year.

Rats are omnivores. This means they eat nuts, berries, fruits and vegetables, as well as birds, fish and reptiles. If they live near humans, they will eat any scraps they find.

Rats can make a lot of
noise. They communicate
by squeaking, hissing,
chattering and grinding
their teeth.

Rats look friendly, but you should not play with them. They can spread diseases through their droppings or by biting people.

What is your favourite fact about this amazing animal?

About The Author

St Columba Animal Series

This book series was written by 4th grade students at St Columba School in Durango, Colorado, with support from Library For All.

The Library For All team ran workshops alongside teaching staff to encourage students and their families to get involved in the book creation process. Students were taught how to research information about animals and how to prepare a book draft for editing.

Library For All works in partnership with authors and illustrators all over the world to create a unique digital library.

www.ingramcontent.com/pod-product-compliance
Lightning Source LLC
Chambersburg PA
CBHW040315050426
42452CB00018B/2856